Isaiah 58:10-11
Feed the hungry, and help those in trouble. Then your light will shine out from the darkness, and the darkness around you will be as bright as noon. The Lord will guide you continually, giving you water when you are dry and restoring your strength. You will be like a well-watered garden, like an ever-flowing spring.

ACKNOWLEDGMENTS

To My Lord and Savior Jesus Christ who showed me I was worthy of Love, Redemption and Restoration. His love is unconditional and without pause. His Grace is without repentance and His Favor and Mercy is non- negotiable

My children Sterling, Cas'ja and Caleb I am blessed to call you my children. You have made me proud of the adults you have become.

To my beautiful grandchildren Taylianna, Josiah, Jo'Sanie and Savier the stars in my eyes, I love you all so much. I am blessed to be your Mimi.

To my Bishops W. Bernard Collier and Maxine Collier, your love and spiritual guidance has allowed me to understand and dig deeper into my relationship with My Lord and Savior. Thank you for your obedience to the call and for serving with such integrity, honor and humbleness. I love you guys so much.

To my Empowerment Center family, thank you for your love, your support and your prayers. You have had my back from the moment I walked through the door as a visitor and now we get to do the Lords work together. In His Service

To my sister Tisha I am so thankful to call you my sister and my confidante. Thank you for your undying support even when others stop believing.

There is no greater feeling than knowing that you are loved for who you are, you don't have to pretend to be flawless for none of us are, I am honored to have the opportunity to do what I am called to do....Inspiring those to live more fulfilling lives and build healthy families and communities.

TABLE OF CONTENT

Introduction	7
Dry Bones	10
Bones of Abandonment	12
Bones of Rejection	26
Bones of Poverty	35
Prayer 1	42
Bones of Depression	43
Prayer	56
Bones of Unworthiness	57
Wisdom Nugget	69
Bones of Insecurity	70
Bones of Self-Loathing	79
Prayer 2	86
Bones of Barren Emotions	87
Dreams Deferred	97

Isaiah 54:10
Though the mountains be shaken, and hills be removed,
Yet my unfailing love for you will not be shaken
Nor my covenant of peace be removed say's the Lord, who has compassion on you

Introduction

One day while listening to Joel Osteen I heard him mention something about dry bones and Ezekiel. I didn't really hear the full message, but those two words stuck out in me. As I continued driving and thinking about my current life, I began praying asking God for his favor and spiritual revelation.

As I veered off to I-16 in Macon, GA, I heard this small voice say read Ezekiel...I have never read Ezekiel and didn't know anything about who Ezekiel was. As a new Christian many years ago, I was taught that our walk was only from the New Testament so for me I never even bothered with reading one scripture from the Old Testament let alone a chapter apart from the Book of Psalms and Proverbs.

I got home and started doing other things and again was reminded to read Ezekiel. I said to self "self, remember to read Ezekiel" didn't happen.

Fast Forward a couple of days and the loving father reminded me again so I listen to Ezekiel 37 and how the Lord spoke to Ezekiel to prophesy to the dry bones. He told Ezekiel to speak to the bones and say *"bones, hear what the Sovereign Lord says I will make breath enter you and you will come to life'. "I will attach tendons to you and make flesh come upon you and cover you with skin; I will put breath in you, and you will come to life then you will know that I am the Lord."*

I envisioned Ezekiel speaking these words to the bones and as they began to take form, I envisioned these bones being connected by the tendons and being bound together by the flesh. I shuttered with the thought that came as I related the dry bones of Ezekiel to the dry bones we carry.

We carry dry bones as monuments of the heartbreak we suffered, bones of rejection, bones of abandonment, bones of unworthiness, bones of insecurity and approval seeking. We carry bones of depression and often lick the bones as a reminder to validate why we carry them.

The Father said that we have the power of life and death in our tongue; we speak life into all things whether they are positive or negative. As he commanded Ezekiel to prophesy to the bones; we have the same power to prophesy to the bones in our lives. We are to speak to those bones and command them to walk; walk right out of your life for good. We don't have to live a life of obscurity or vacant of love, success and joy.

We have the power within ourselves to bring about the things we so desire, but it takes belief. Belief in the father that his promises belong to us and belief within ourselves that we can accomplish the things we want and that we are worthy of receiving the very things we desire.

In the course of our journey through life we all will suffer great loss, pain and triumph. We watch those closes to us in order to learn how to navigate through the obstacles and barriers of life. There are those of us who have seen the worse that life has to offer and have decided that there is nothing more to life than pain and disappointment. They wake up every day thinking the same vibration of pain, clothe in the same garment of disappointment and sending the same stench of animosity and negativity to their environment even though the sun has set on the old and a new day is present.

No, I'm not saying that there is no valid reason behind feeling what you feel. Nor am I saying that it should or could be ignored but it does mean that if what has happen is out of your control. Then holding on to the pain of life and reliving it daily means that you have chosen to remain in the place where pain and disappointment resides.

When life happens in the form of death of a spouse, illness, divorce, it can take the wind out of us and leave us with many questions as to why this happen to us or what did I do to deserve this. We question the meaning of life when we suffer the unimaginable pain of life. And yes, it is valid to feel what you feel. But you can't stay there, you can't inflict the pain you feel onto well-meaning people who cross your path to bring you hope, experience or a shoulder to unload the boulder that holds you down. Being a person that spews venom onto others pushes others away and that's when the isolation begins.

Even though there are those that result to the above mention there are those who go through every roadblock and obstacle that comes upon them, yet they find a way to go through it and put it in its proper place, they don't allow it to turn them contemptuous. They choose to although suffering from the pain they walk through life achieving their idea of success but are held down by carrying their dry bones in their heart and mind.

Dry Bones!

In the bible God transported Ezekiel the prophet in a vision to the Valley of Dry Bones. He told Ezekiel to prophesy to those bones and tell the bones that "God was going to make breathe into them and they will live". Ezekiel obeyed and the bones came to life, flesh covered and tendons connected. The bones stood up as an army ready to fight. Ezekiel 37

The dry bones that lay in the valley of our heart and minds are the heart breaks of life that we have allowed to lay dead in our lives. The bones of rejection, abandonment, poverty, depression, insecurity, anger and unworthiness lay in the depth of our heart and sabotages the life that God breath in us to have.

We allow these dry bones to give life to the pain and brokenness and we carry them into relationship after relationship and we wonder what is wrong with the other person when in fact it is the valley we have taken up residence in.

My bones of rejection, abandonment, and unworthiness took a large part of my life for many years. I walked in the shadows of life because I never felt worthy enough to stand out. As a child I was rejected by my parents due to them not knowing how to handle their own rejections. I suffered emotional abandonment my entire childhood and it shaped me into a person who never felt like I measured up to anyone.

As with many people we find things to excel in that will give us an image of acceptance but in the dark rooms of our minds we really believe that we don't fit in. Some of us will sabotage relationships seeking perfection from someone who cannot possibly meet those expectations. We insist on them reaching the unreachable because subconsciously we use this to confirm to our inner self that no one can be trusted with our hearts. But the reality is we do this to keep from exposing ourselves to potential pain and we leave behind us a trail of broken hearted people who now live in the shadows of doubting who they are.

Although I suffered a tremendous amount of rejection in my life from family, friends and significant others I am understanding that because I have carried these bones for so long I looked at life through the lenses of brokenness and because of how I saw life I attracted the very thing that validated my unworthiness. I attracted those who were emotionally unavailable and tried to get them to approve of me when in actuality they could not because of their own lack of self-approval.

The saying "hurt people hurt people" well broken people break people….

I have spoken to the dry bones in my life and have commanded them to walk…I hope that this book will speak to the areas in your life that are dry and you will let the those bones walk out of your life;.

It is my prayer that we all live a life free from feelings of unworthiness, abandonment, rejection, depression and poverty.

Bones of Abandonment
Duet 31:6

Be strong and of good courage, do not fear nor be afraid of them; for the Lord your God, He is the One who goes with you. He will not leave you nor forsake you.

****
***

Abandonment: to leave completely and finally; to give up, discontinue, withdraw from

The Fear of Abandonment typically stems from a childhood loss, loss to a traumatic event, loss of a parent to death or divorce. Fear of Abandonment also occurs from not getting enough physical or emotional care. For many being chained to the fear of abandonment we believe that we are in danger of being personally rejected, discarded or replace. These feelings come upon us in any and all relationships whether we are a parent and fear that our children will love their teachers, coaches or best friend parent more than us. Or a love one who will see someone that has more to offer them and they will choose this individual over us.

Fear of Abandonment will have us feeling that no one of great status will really want to be with us and if they do we sabotage the relationship or seek retribution for something that is not present. Abandonment will often manifest itself in the form of jealousy and accuse others of unfaithfulness because we lack deficiency of object constancy.

Object Constancy is having the ability to understand that people and things remain constant even when you can't see them or verify that they are there. This is a challenge for those who have experienced abandonment and haven't processed through it effectively.

When someone experiences chronic loss such as being denied physical and psychological protection, one can internalize the loss and by not receiving the necessary physical or psychological protection. This lack equals abandonment which if not processed correctly leads to toxic shame. Shame sends a pain message that says "you are not worthy', "you are not important" "you are nothing".

Emotional Abandonment

Emotional abandonment or neglect is traumatic and can leave deep seeded wounds that mask themselves in various ways.

Emotional abandonment can occur when parents:
- Stifle their children's emotional expression
- Ridicule their children
- Hold their children to standards that are too high
- Rely too heavily on children for their own sense of worth
- Treat their children as peers

Adults who have suffered emotional abandonment as a child will create barriers and walls to their heart to avoid being hurt. Adults of emotional abandonment suffer low self-esteem, relationship issues, fear of intimacy, depression and/or codependency.

The psychological effects of abandonment stretches over into low self-esteem in which one will strive to be perfect and expect perfection from his or her partner. Some will avoid conflict so intensely that they will evade important conversation for fear of feeling uneasy and uncomfortable. Many people grow up with fears around abandonment. Some are plagued by these fears pretty consistently throughout their lives.

They worry they'll be rejected by peers, partners, schools, companies, or entire social circles. For many others, these fears aren't fully realized until they enter into a romantic relationship. Things will be going along smoothly, and all of a sudden, they feel inundated with insecurity and dread that their partner will distance themselves, ignore, or leave them.

Everyone experiences this fear at different levels. Most of us can relate to having heightened anxiety over thoughts of rejection and abandonment. In extreme cases, some people become overwhelmed with the fear of being alone or isolated.

When one fears being alone and isolated, they then perceive themselves as being ignored, or uncared even when they're with the other person. They may also experience a fear of abandonment phobia, which is characterized by extreme dependency on others. They rely heavily on their partner to validate their self-worth. Because they grew up insecure which was based on the inconsistent availability of their caregivers, they will anticipate rejection or abandonment and will sabotage the relationship by withdrawing, cheating or ghosting.

The degree to which a person is faced with this fear can shape how they live their lives and experience their relationships. Adults who experience a fear of abandonment may struggle with a preoccupied attachment style. They may feel triggered by even subtle or imagined signs of rejection from their partner. As a result, they may act possessive, controlling, jealous, or clingy toward their partner. Some will display distrust and jump to another relationship. Interesting fact about this fear is one will become dependent, or make unreasonable demands and act possessive which tends to backfire and bring about the very abandonment that they fear.

There are those who have abandonment fears and act in punishing, resentful, and angry ways when their partner doesn't give them the attention they believe they need to feel secure.

This schema continues over and over until the individual heals from the wounds of the past and let go of the bone of abandonment.

Life Work:

Abandonment issues are reversible it takes a strong commitment to yourself to work through the pain but it is worth it in order to have the successful life that the Lord has promised to you.

Trust: this is a big change but requires small and necessary steps to be taken in order to live a complete life of real freedom. The idea of trusting someone again can be a bit overwhelming because you have to make yourself open up to the risk.

- Confiding in a person about something in your life that no one knows about is a great first step. This person should be someone you admire and have a closeness already established. Taking this step will strengthen your friendship and allow you the comfort of going further.

- Find an outlet to help process your thoughts. For many journaling is a perfect way to process your feelings and thoughts as you learn to trust again. Women who turn to their creative sides will find this to be a very helpful way to process. Men who take up a sport including fishing or hone certain hobbies can be very useful when thoughts emerge and the impulse to pull away comes in like a flood. It is imperative to find that outlet as well as the sharing with a friend/love one as you win over the fear.

- Owning your feelings it can be so easy to hide in the comfort of denial and not really accept that anything feels scary or worrying. While this may feel comfortable for a little while, it doesn't do us any favors in terms of moving forward with our lives. Instead of jumping to cover up or hide your feelings lets own them and be not ashamed that we have acted or feel the way we do. It's natural to feel nervous or hesitant when it comes to meeting new people or attempting to engage in a commitment. We all self-sabotage sometimes in order to avoid fully immersing ourselves in experiences. Whenever a negative feeling arises, don't immediately brush it away. Consider what it means and what has triggered it, maybe looking at old photos made you remember a discomforting time or speaking hearing from someone in your past just as you beginning a new relationship. By learning what makes us feel certain ways, we can start working toward surrounding ourselves with positivity and support.

Journal:

Take the first steps to healing physically and mentally. The Lord has healed you already we just have to walk in that healing:

1. Name your origin of fear?

2. How has holding on to this fear kept you from living complete?

3. Write down all that you have lost due to fear_____

   _____
   _____
   _____
   _____
   _____
   _____
   _____
   _____
   _____
   _____
   _____
   _____
   _____
   _____
   _____
   _____
   _____
   _____
   _____
   _____
   _____
   _____
   _____
   _____
   _____ .

4. Name two people you know you can confide in and why?_____

5. Look in the mirror and tell yourself why you trust yourself? If this is uncomfortable for you to do write down why it's uncomfortable._____

6. Write down five declarations that you will say to yourself every day to remind yourself that you are no longer bound by the fear of abandonment..

1.

2.

3.

4.

5

2
Bones of Rejection
John 14:18, Romans 8:16

We are no longer orphans, but have been adopted into His kingdom as His children.

****

In the bible the 2nd chapter of Genesis you read that God says "it is not good for man to be alone" At which point he created Eve from the rib of Adam. From the very beginning of our existence we were created to bond, share and thrive with one another. The human heart is delicate but strong as it circulates the blood through the body providing nutrients and oxygen to the organs to perform at its optimal best just as the father intended it to be at creation.

But when the heart is not operating at full capacity the body becomes weak and can eventually cause death. Rejection can cause the death of ones self-esteem and self-worth, it
knows no bounds, invading social, romantic and job situations alike. And it feels terrible because it communicates that we are not loved, not wanted, nor are we of value.

Rejection undermines our need to be a part of something or someone. We all have a fundamental need to belong it's the reason why so many settled for unhealthy relationships, we need to feel that we are important even if we are pretending.

When we are rejected the disconnection we feel adds to our emotional pain. Reconnecting with those who love us, or reaching out to people we feel a strong affinity for and who value and accept us, has been found to soothe emotional pain after a rejection.

However, it is very difficult for the rejected to take the first step to reach out to someone when they are fighting off the overwhelming feeling of lack of worth and value.

The feeling of being alone and disconnected after a rejection, has an often overlooked impact on our behavior. Rejections send us on a subconscious mission to seek and destroy our self-esteem. We often respond to romantic rejections by finding fault in ourselves, bemoaning all our inadequacies, kicking ourselves when we're already down, and smacking our self-esteem into a pulp by making unhealthy and risky decisions in order to soothe the pain.

The risky behaviors that occur can be anything from drug abuse to risky sex lives trying to prove our value. We look to others to validate our being when in fact we have already been validated by the Lord. Romantic relationships are the closes we come to feeling complete here on earth. Society says that if you are not married or in a committed relationship then something must be wrong. This way of thinking further ignites the pain of rejection.

We often don't realize that romantic rejections are a matter of a poor fit and a lack of chemistry. If we are really honest with ourselves we will admit that we settled and disregarded the things that were not present and accepted less than in order to be in a relationship. We will ignore this voice and self-mutilate our worth by being with someone who doesn't really care or respect us. We accept moments of physical pleasure and use it to say it is love.

If we do not process rejection and place it in its proper place we will begin to expect it all the time which can lead to self-rejection. When we don't process rejection correctly we tend to allow it to drop our feelings of self-worth

Everyone is sensitive to rejection and we all have experienced it at some point in our lives. When people have experienced rejection of any kind they tend to avoid any situation that will cause them to experience it again which then puts them at a higher risk for loneliness and/or become emotionally unavailable. Emotional unavailable people are those who have suffered abandonment or rejections. This person might have commitment issues and tend to run the moment they feel another person is getting to close, they might have self-esteem issues and worry that if you are interested in them that something must be wrong with you, or they might not be an especially nice, kind or sensitive person to be with. Their tart attitude may be a direct link to their bitterness towards their unresolved rejection. Remember the person being rejected did nothing wrong to cause the rejection nor did it have anything to do with inadequacies. If someone gives you the "it's not you, It's me" line. Believe them it is not you it is them.

Life Work
- Rejection has nothing to do with the person being rejected. It has everything to do with the wounds of the other person both known and unknown. Many people hurt others by not being completely open and honest with one another.
- Parents who reject their children often do so without realizing that the life trap they are repeating comes directly from their own residue of rejection. In order to understand the present state of rejection one must visit the past rejection and leave it in the past.

Journal
1. List any negative or self-critical thoughts you have about yourself?

_____
_____
_____
_____
_____
_____
_____
_____
_____
_____
_____
_____
_____
_____
_____
_____

2. Explain where are these thoughts coming from? _____

3. Make a list of five characteristics, attributes or traits you value highly that you possess within yourself._____

4. Rank your list of characteristic according to their order of importance to you.

5. Choose two of the top three attributes you listed and write a short essay about each one, covering the following points.

- Why the specific quality is important to you

- How does having this quality influence your life

- Why is this quality and important part of your life

Essay:

3
Bones of Poverty
Psalm 34:6 (NIV)

This poor man called, and the Lord listened; he saved him from all his troubles

****

Poverty: the state of being inferior, extremely poor

If the word says that the Lord hears our prayers and answers them, then why is there an overwhelming percentage in poverty? Many people spend hours and days fasting for the relief of the poor that envelopes our world. The word of God is true regardless of our situation and Jesus said that the poor will always be with us.

Poverty is not only a state of being but it is state of mind and heart. We look at the bible and it says in Matt 26:11 "the poor you will always have with you" If this is the case then can we really end poverty? Poverty is not just about food and shelter but poverty is also of the soul.

In *Jeremiah 4:22* **"*My people are fools; they do not know me, they are senseless children; they have no understanding, they are skilled in doing evil; they know not how to do good"*.**

Today, we see the work of this scripture in our children who have no empathy or compassion for one another. Adults who live their lives using others, hurting one another just because they feel that they have a right do so. We see teenagers bullying one another and posting videos of it on social media which pushes their victims to the point of suicide. We have adults buying and selling our children for sex like they are buying groceries.

In our society we see the most profound examples of poverty of the soul. It is the residue of a community that has lost faith and trust in the government, the church, family and in themselves. So many people are looking for life to have meaning and because they can't find it they act out in extremely inappropriate and dangerous ways.

We all have seen a young boy who has picked up a weapon and killed an innocent victim. Our young women with body image difficulties will tolerate being in abusive relationship because they have become numb to the voice that says this is not love. Our young people are being raised by individuals who have lost hope in the good and are planting hopeless seeds in the next generation. What we see in our community is that this generation is dying off physically after having already allowed their hope to die.

We all feel a longing deep down in our soul for something more. We want to be heard, we want to be understood and supported. We all want to feel that we matter to someone. We all want to have the joy of knowing that life is good because we can laugh and enjoy the smell of comfort, so many of us are disheartened because we can't find this anywhere.

We are not finding it in our community leaders or in our political leaders, we have been left to deal with the poverty of the soul by cosigning on with others that we see who have lost just as much hope as the next.

It is not just the job of the spiritual leaders to meet the spiritual need of the hurting. But we all should take responsibility for connecting with others and helping them and restoring hope in their eyes and their lives. We can regain hope if we learn to have compassion and empathy for one another.

We are so caught up in status quo that we have forgotten about the charge to care for the orphans and widows. Who are the orphans? They are not just children but the orphan is anyone that has been left to their own devices with the lack of knowledge, provisions and/or love.

We have to elevate our thinking past the poverty of food and shelter and realize that the poor among us is not only those poor in income but poor in soul. There are so many people walking through life hopeless, they have lost hope in family, friends and the church. The pain and heartbreak suffered through life has crushed the spirit and we see the results today.

When was the last time we hugged someone or picked up the phone to say "hey what can I do for you". When was the last time that you saw someone homeless and you bought them a meal? Or you bought groceries for a single mother or offered to watch her kids so she can rest.

The world we live in today if full of broken people who need someone to show they care regardless of their flaws. We have to take the time to show others how valuable they are. Everyone was given a gift, talent, and a special skill. We have to change how we think. We have to risk showing care and love for the sake of the souls that are currently lost.

As a whole, society is lacking the proper nourishment to combat the consequence of the broken souls that exist in our youth and the hopelessness in adults who struggle to find meaning and peace.

It is easy to judge someone for their lack of education, money, status and upbringing. It's easy to deflect our own private lack while we expose others. If we are to change our homes, our church and our community; we have to look at ways to nourish and not with food but with compassion, nurturing, empathy, discipline and humility We all have a lack in something that can be debilitating at some time or another.

Essay:

In what area of your life are you poor? Be honest with yourself.

Who can you help today? Name 4 people and what you can do for them

Poverty is a state of mind, there are many who live in what we may call a poverty state but they fill as though they are the riches people on earth. Their value is not in material things but in the freedom to love one self and to be able to be at peace with those in their lives.

We do not have to agree with everyone around us but we can surely choose to be happy and not remain broken and in despair day to day.

Prayer

Father,

As I ponder the wonders of who you are. I can't begin to fathom the kind of love you have for me. I have suffered many disappointments, rejections, abandonment and heartache and in those seasons I made some big mistakes and even walked away from your will. Many times I wanted to cry out but I didn't know if you would listen to me, now I know that your love for me is truly unconditional, your grace is perfect in the storm and your mercy unfailing for the ones you love.

Father, I don't know how you will cleanse me of all that I have inside but I do know that only you can heal my brokenness, seal the wounds and create a temple for you to dwell in within my heart.

I don't know the perfect words to say but I am going to trust that you know and see my heart. I ask you Father to come into my heart, renew my heart ad my mind. Create in me a clean heart and cover me with your love and your grace.

Heal me of anything I have said or done, cleanse me that I have right standing with you.

I believe you gave your life for me and you choose me from the creation. I have been bought with a price and that price was your life. So I ask you to take over and dwell in me.

In Jesus Name…Amen

4

Bones of Depression
Psalm 40:1-3

I waited patiently and expectantly for the Lord; And He inclined to me and heard my cry.2 He brought me up out of a horrible pit [of tumult and of destruction], out of the miry clay, and He set my feet upon a rock, steadying my footsteps and establishing my path. 3 He put a new song in my mouth, a song of praise to our God; Many will see and fear [with great reverence] And will trust confidently in the Lord.

****

Some 15 million Americans a year struggle with depression, an illness that comes in many forms—from major depression and seasonal affective disorder, to dysthymia and bipolar disorder.

Depression is an illness that increasingly afflicts people worldwide, interfering with concentration, motivation and many other aspects of everyday functioning. It is a complex disorder, involving many systems of the body, including the immune system, either as cause or effect. It disrupts sleep, and it interferes with appetite, in some cases causing weight loss, in others weight gain. Because of its complexity, a full understanding of depression has been elusive.

Dealing with depression needs action but taking action can seem so depilating. Thinking about doing the very things that will make you feel better can be exhausting in itself. However, doing the very thing that will help rid you from the state of depression always takes the most effort to put them in action. Taking the first step is always the hardest. But dancing to your favorite song or taking a walk will boost your energy which serves as a defense against the depression fog.

What is Depression really? Depression really is a mood disorder; it is much more than sadness that's due to life struggles and setbacks. It affects how you think, function and feel. It invades your ability to work, sleep, study, eat and enjoy life. Feeling helpless and worthless can be so intense that many feel they can't go on . For some suffering with depression you can feel lifeless, unimportant, lack self-love and shut off from the world. It is important to remember that these are symptoms of depression they are not the reality of your life.

Symptoms of Depression

Not everyone who is depressed or manic experiences every symptom. Some people experience a few symptoms, some many. Severity of symptoms varies among individuals and also varies over time.

- Persistent sad, anxious, or empty mood
- Feelings of hopelessness or pessimism
- Feelings of guilt, worthlessness, or helplessness
- Loss of interest or pleasure in hobbies and activities that were once enjoyed, including sex
- Decreased energy, fatigue, being "slowed down"
- Difficulty concentrating, remembering, or making decisions
- Insomnia, early morning awakening or oversleeping
- Appetite and/or weight loss, or overeating and weight gain
- Thoughts of death or suicide, suicide attempts
- Restlessness, irritability
- Persistent physical symptoms that do not respond to treatment, such as headaches, digestive disorders and chronic pain

Causes of Depression

There is no single known cause of depression. Rather, it likely results from a combination of genetic, biochemical, environmental, and psychological factors. Trauma, loss of a loved one, a difficult relationship, or any stressful situation that overwhelms the ability for one to cope may trigger a depressive episode. Subsequent depressive episodes may occur with or without an obvious trigger.

Moving out of the depression fog

At times you may feel too exhausted to talk, ashamed at your situation, or guilty for neglecting certain relationships. But this is just the depression talking. You have to move outside the fog to get relief from the darkness that tries to drown you. Some may feel that reaching out to others make them appear weak or that you are a burden to them. But the people in your life care deeply about you and want to help anyway they know how. There are some who have alienated family and friends with their disposition and negative outlook on life.

Taking the first step is the hardest but once you have taking the step towards freeing yourself from the hold of depression, you will see yourself in a better light and in turn others will see the light in you.

Things to do to step out
- ✓ Make face-time a priority- social media and texting are great ways to stay in touch. But nothing can replace face to face contact. Seeing someone's smile, feeling their warmth helps alleviate depression.
- ✓ Keep up with social activities even if you don't like it- when you are depressed you feel better in your shell but others help you feel less depressed. Their energy is contagious…
- ✓ Get moving- get out of bed, off the couch and move. Even if it's a stroll down your street or exercising in your living room. The goal is to move for at least 30 mins a day but this does not have to been done all at once you can take 10 mins at a time. The point is to move.
- ✓ Add positive elements to your thoughts- if you depression is rooted in resolved trauma you have to rethink all your thoughts to move pass the negativity. You have to be purposeful to think on positive things in order to change the elements of your thoughts.

- ✓ Develop a wellness toolbox here are some suggestions to put in your box
    - Spend some time in nature
    - List what you like about yourself
    - Read a good book or two
    - Take a long hot bath or shower
    - Listen to uplifting music
    - Do something spontaneous

Add 5 more things to list that you can reach for when you need too

1. What was the one event in your life that has caused your depressive state?

_____
_____
_____
_____
_____
_____
_____
_____
_____
_____
_____
_____
_____
_____
_____
_____
_____
_____
_____
_____
_____

2. Describe your perfect day, who would you spend it with and what would you do?

3. Write down 3 things that trigger feelings of depression in you, write down how you can combat them.

4. Write a letter to your teenage self telling him/her what you wish he/she knew

5. Discuss something that you wish others knew about you.

6. What songs help lift your spirits when you are feeling down?

7. If you could change ONE thing about you what would it be and why?

8. What do you want to feel tomorrow and what 3 things can you do today to ensure you feel these things tomorrow?

Prayer

Father,

You created our minds to be the most powerful organ in our body along with our heart. One does not function properly if the other is broken. Our minds can create something out of nothing just by the sheer thought of it. However, to often the things we create with our mind our negative and debilitating things. When we suffer pain we allow our minds to hold on to the pain as a way to protect us from another painful event. What we don't realize is that by holding to the pain does not allow you to have the freedom of release and healing in our lives'

Father,

Today I come to you with hope and with thanksgiving. I know you are God and although I have not asked you into my life. I come to you this day asking for your presences to rein in my life. I ask that you send forth the Holy Spirit to assist me in living out loud the assignment you have on my life. I was made with a purpose, you created me to do great things and on this day I acknowledge that and I thank you. Forgive me for hurting myself and others with my words or deeds. Renew my heart and my mind to bring forth the gifts that are within me that I may live a life of fulfillment, purpose and freedom.

It is in Jesus Name I ask this…Amen

Date:_____

5
Bones of Unworthiness
Psalm 139:1-3 13

For you formed my innermost parts; You knit me [together] in my mother's womb. 14 I will give thanks and praise to you, for I am fearfully and wonderfully made; Wonderful are your works, And my soul knows it very well. 15 My frame was not hidden from you, when I was being formed in secret, and intricately and skillfully formed [as if embroidered with many colors] in the depths of the earth. 16 Your eyes have seen my unformed substance; And in Your book were all written the days that were appointed for me, When as yet there was not one of them [even taking shape).

****

If you're sitting around feeling like you really don't measure up, know that it's not all that uncommon to experience a feeling of unworthiness on occasion.

For some, this occurs when trying to measure up to the unrealistic expectations others have for us. And the debilitating expectations we place on ourselves knowing that they are far reaching yet we do so to validate the unworthiness we feel within. For many of us, however, we most feel unworthy when we are overwhelmed by an intense emotional feeling for one person and, due to a variety of reasons, we feel that we just aren't worthy of that person's love and affection or even their respect or admiration.

The truth is that holding onto such negative emotion is completely counter-productive. Not only does it do nothing in the moment to change anything, it also has a cumulative negative effect on the body and the mind. The more you believe you are unworthy, the less you think of yourself. Consequently, the less you think of yourself the more you neglect relationships because of the fear, shame or guilt, and you internalize all this negativity to the point where your body suffers medically as well as psychological consequences.

Consider the fact that everyone experiences unworthiness at one point or another. So, it isn't the feeling of being unworthy that should cause concern but the inability to deal with such feelings when they do occur. What is the cause of your thought of unworthiness? What has happen in your life that you feel you do not measure up as an average person?

No one is perfect. No matter whom you are or what you've achieved in life in terms of financial gain, prestige, fame, number of friends, or material possessions, sometime you're going to feel inadequate.

What can you do to get past this decidedly uncomfortable and potentially debilitating feeling?

Acknowledge what you feel

If you are feeling like you are unworthy and not sure why; this feeling can resonate from different events that have occurred in your life. It could be you have an issue with trust. It's possible that you have been betrayed by the person of the opposite sex, or just let down. And you have not process those feelings and they have been left them to merge into your core belief which has been contaminated with betrayal and/or rejection.

Our worth does not come from another person, we are all born with human worth the moment we enter this world. Human worth means that we are important and valuable as a person because we are unique, precious and have unchanging value. We all have unconditional worth as a person. Worth is not comparative or competitive. Although you may have someone that is better in sports, or have a nice figure or even has a striking beauty. Their worth is no more valuable than yours. We all have something that another does not have. The difference is the thought process. If we think we are not worthy then we act like we are not worthy. Let's look at celebrities who get paid for their looks. They have a look that will sell a product or an idea; it does not mean they are more worthy than you or I. It only means they have an external that they can use to get monetary gains.

Externals neither add nor diminish our internal value or internal growth. Externals include things like looks, money, performance and achievements. These things only increase social worth not over all worth. Our core self is where our worth lies. Our core is surrounded by externals and some externals can hide the core, while other externals brighten our core. The love of others helps us *feel* our worth, our talent that is shared with others is a way we *express* our worth. Our externals change the way our worth is experienced not our worth itself.

Some people spend their lives trying to look good on the outside to cover up shame, or a feeling of worthlessness, on the inside. If, however we spend our time using externals to fill the empty feelings at the core we will always be unfulfilled, unhappy and always seeking the approval of others and things to fill the voids in us, It is not possible to earn core worth from things, others or performance. Although the messages we receive from TV programming and societies push for material possession and status. It is difficult at times to separate the externals from the core without deliberate thoughts.

The messages that we receive from programming is if we are not a certain size, skin tone, wealthy or young then we are worthless.

If we don't belong to a particular church or denomination then we are wrong and don't belong.

If we are not married then there is something wrong with us and therefore not worthy of respect or value.

If we live in a certain part of town then we are looked down on and not given the necessary tools and resources.

There are many symptoms of feeling unworthy; here are some symptoms this list does not exhaust the symptoms one may feel with battling unworthiness.

* Self-esteem issues that make you feel unworthy of being loved.
* Have fear of being jilted, or being used.
* Are 'programmed' (psychologically been beaten down), not loved, respected or appreciated by your parents, friends, etc. and consider yourself to be unworthy of love and respect.
* Fear pain and rejection.
* Have limiting self-beliefs.

The veils of unworthiness

The primary trance-inducing veil is fear-based thinking. When we're stuck in fear-based thinking we are driven by paralyzing fear that we are not good enough or we are not smart enough. This thought process is based on our own self condemnation, as well as the need to succeed or dominate in order to feel that we have value in the world. We act out in inappropriate and destructive ways. The more we do this, the deeper our trance of unworthiness becomes.

The unworthiness stems from the lack of self appreciation and the self-defeating thoughts we allow to run continuously, as we look for ways to deflect the thoughts, we began looking for someone to say we are worthy and to validate our existence.

We allow the negative automatic thoughts to determine how we react to life and how we see ourselves. We are inundated with messages of who we should be at different milestones in our lives. There are messages that say we should be thin, thick, brown or white. We are sent messages from the media that says if we do not have a certain type of car or a certain kind of house then we are not accepted. It is ok to strive for the desires of your heart because God is the focus of your drive. But when we say we are not worthy or feel unworthy because of what someone else says, we then tell God that he was wrong in creating us. And he is never wrong, EVER.

Romans 12:2(Holy Bible) and be not conformed to this world; but be ye transformed by the renewing of your mind, that ye may prove what is good, and acceptable, and perfect, will of God.

We are not to allow the world to tell us who we are. Whether you are a faithful believer or not a believer at all, you are not to grant others permission to shape your worth.

We have all suffered some unimaginable things in our lives and even the worst violation does not erase the value we have. You are an overcomer and have the inner strength to climb over obstacles that will attempt to keep you stuck.

There is nothing that you can't overcome if you look to the inner strength that is in you. So many messages tell us to work on our weakness to make us whole. But what if we change that mindset and work on showing our strength instead of highlighting our weakness we will start to see confidence rise and our self-respect increase.

If you continue to walk around in an emotional fog, knowing that you feel "unworthy" it's hard to see yourself valuable and if we don't see ourselves as valuable we will continue attracting those who don't treat us as valuable.

Journal:

Think back to a highpoint or an experience in your life in which you were at your best

_____
_____
_____
_____
_____
_____
_____
_____
_____
_____
_____
_____
_____
_____
_____
_____
_____

What condition empowered you to be at your best?_____

_____
_____
_____
_____

Being you best you can only come when you are true to yourself and love yourself as human being. Your worth is not in the value of your home, cars, career or status of your mate.

Your worth is what you are regardless of those things, in fact you make those things not the other way around.

Below is a list of twenty-four character strengths. Pick seven that resonate within you?

****

1. Appreciation of beauty and excellence
2. Gratitude
3. Forgiveness
4. Hope
5. Humor
6. Diligence
7. Judgment
8. Open minded
9. Leadership
10. Teamwork
11. Loyal
12. Love of learning
13. Fairness
14. Justice minded
15. Capacity to love
16. Brave
17. Self- Control
18. Authentic
19. Energy
20. Social Intelligence
21. Sense of Purpose
22. Humble
23. Mercy
24. Open to love
25. Creative

Now pick your top 3 and write why you think these are your top three?
1.

2.

3.

4. Pretend you are meeting someone for the first time and you are doing an introduction. Below write your introduction of yourself and include a time when you had to exhibit strength to handle a challenging moment in your life.

5. Imagine that you are talking to an individual who is completely blind. They ask you to describe how you look. Write exactly how you look being totally honest with yourself.

We are all worthy and full of desirable traits. We have to believe that we are attractive, smart, positive and full of joy and life. There are no mistakes in who we were created to be.

We are a workmanship created in love.

6
Bones of Insecurity:
Ephesians 2: 10

For we are his workmanship, created in Christ Jesus for good works, which God prepared beforehand, that we should walk in them

****

Most people seek a soul mate to love them unconditionally. But those who need such acceptance most are the terminally insecure who often sabotage their own chances at bliss. When we're feeling low, we often gain confidence through a partners love and support. People who suffer from low self-esteem assume that their love ones notice their glaring faults and will eventually reject them or withhold affection from them.

People with low self-esteem are at a greater risk of feeling vulnerable in a relationship. They tend to believe their partner's regard is conditional, where as stable relationships are known to boost self-esteem.

Through interactions with empathic caregivers, children learn about their emotional worlds, their own worth and capabilities or in too many cases a lack of worth. Through these interactions we learn whether we can trust ourselves and other people. Securely attached adults most likely experienced empathic and soothing interactions with caregivers as children and are able to express their emotions freely. They are able to make sense of, understand, and communicate their own emotions and experience empathy for others.

Insecure Attachment

Insecurely attached adults have a more disconnected brain. They tend to avoid their own emotions and feel uncomfortable with the closeness and other people's emotions. Insecure attached adults become flooded with intense emotions when they are under stress, that they act impulsively and are less able to do logical problem-solving.

Many insecure adults choose the same types of unhealthy partners over and over again (rigid pattern), or exhaust themselves using every strategy at their disposal to try to control their romantic partners or keep them from leaving (chaotic pattern).

If things are not going our way, perhaps it is because circumstances are leading us on a different path. If we have the courage to try new ways of thinking and behaving, we might be pleasantly surprised by how things turn out.

No one would say that they set out to get into a relationship with an insecure person. However, that's exactly what many of us do with majority of these being women. An insecure man can be tempting particularly if he is expressing his undying love and affection when the last relationship was with a man who did not value you and was selfish and a bottomless pit that drained you of every drop of love you possess.

We often move into the next relationship with out processing what we allowed in the previous relationship and we expect subconsciously and at time consciously for the next one to pay the price for the previous one. We tend to make others live out a sentence that does not belong to them. We are aware of what we are doing especially when we say "men are all dogs" yet we want a man in our lives. We can't expect new and different if we go into it with the old and same mentality.

. If we do not allow ourselves to heal from the pain of the past we will continue to live an insecure life and drag along innocent bystanders on our journey if we continue to think we are ok and everyone else is wrong and out to hurt us.

Truthfully speaking when we are dating while wounded we are looking through tainted eyes and we ignore signs and behaviors of an insecure man/woman in order for us to fill the lonely void we have. We place ourselves in vulnerable positions by ignoring the signs that an insecure person will exhibit.

Insecure individuals can come in any package: rich, poor, short, tall, attractive or unattractive. They can be well educated and or high school dropout. Insecurity has no boundaries and will merge into anyone's life regardless of status. Insecure people seek unhealthy validation and attention from those in their circle and those who are not. Insecure people are critical, judgmental, extremely jealous and very manipulative. They will alienate you from friends and family only to keep you under their control and that is mainly because they are insecure within themselves that they cannot see you happy outside of them.

Most people who are insecure do not know when they are exhibiting deal breaker behaviors. And those that are aware of it will never admit to it in most cases and if they do they will claim "this is who I am ".

Insecurity is shown in some subtle ways like eye contact. Insecure men have difficulty maintaining eye contact with anyone. They typically feel that looking someone in the eyes is uncomfortable and are concern that someone will detect their insecurities. Insecure women will hold grudges or have jealous periods and have impulses to check phones or emails. These signs are not peg to one gender for depending on the individuals the signs can swap genders.

Some men are known to hold a grudge as some women are known not to give eye contact especially those who feel unworthy as well as dealing with insecurity.

The following are a couple of key signs of an insecure man:

- ❖ Needing Constant Reassurance
- ❖ Approval
- ❖ Smothering
- ❖ Jealous and Possessive
- ❖ Distrustful
- ❖ Jealous

- ❖ Dishonest
- ❖ Extremely introverted
- ❖ Avoids direct eye contact

The following are a couple of key signs of an insecure woman:

- ❖ Defensive
- ❖ Control
- ❖ Jealous
- ❖ Belittle
- ❖ Needy reinforcement
- ❖ Spell of insecurity
- ❖ Grudges
- ❖ Spell of guilt/shame

Who are you in your adult relationships? Do you struggle with a deep-seeded insecurity? Do you regularly question your self-worth when it comes to love?

Attachment anxiety manifests in romantic relationships in a variety of ways. People with more attachment anxiety might be called "needy" in their relationships; they have trouble balancing independence with closeness. Instead of being content and trusting, individuals high in anxiety are constantly striving for connection and attention (e.g., excessive texting) and might engage in strategic behaviors (e.g., to make a partner jealous) to elicit proof of their partner's love.

"What ruins relationships and causes most fights is insecurity" — Olivia Wilde

Secure love can be "earned" through openness and trusting efforts. There are no easy fixes to building secure love but it is essential to having a joyous and prosperous relationship. Many of us who battle insecurity have a difficult time trusting the Lord because the root cause of insecurity is lack of self-worth and self-love. Insecurity is an inner feeling of being threatened and/or inadequate in some way.

People tend to think that insecurity comes from something their partner said or did; the reality is that *most* insecurity comes from inside of our selves. The feeling can start early in life with an insecure attachment to your parents, or can develop after being hurt or rejected by someone you care about. When insecurity drives our actions in relationships we create dysfunction and deflect it to the person we are insecure towards.

Good News!
We don't have to live wrapped in the pain of insecurity.
Following are steps we can take to destroy insecurity for good in our lives.

Psalms 118:9 (NLT): It is better to take refuge in the Lord than to trust in princes.

Defeating insecurity:
1. **Find your own value**

There too many people that allow others to shape their value instead of conforming to what others say we should be. We need to discover our own value, most of the time when we are feeling insecure, we are often focused on something we feel is lacking about ourselves.

In order to feel more secure in any relationship it helps to know what you have to offer and you discover this by knowing your own value. Your value is not about the material things you own, the kind of career you have or even how physically fit you are.

Your personality is much more important in a relationship.

What traits do you have? Name 5

1._____

2._____

3._____

4._____

5._____

The traits you listed far exceed money in any healthy relationship.

Now answer these questions?

In your relationship how do you make them feel loved, supported, and happy?_____

These are things everyone wants to feel in a relationship, but many often don't. Focus on what you offer instead of what you feel you lack; this will change your perspective. If the other person doesn't appreciate what you have to offer, that's his or her loss. We can't make a person love us all we can do is be our authentic self and trust that the person we love will appreciate who we are and love us authentically.

2. Develop self-esteem

When you aren't feeling good about who you are on the inside, it is natural to want to look outside of yourself for validation. However, trying to feel good by getting approval from your partner, boss or friend is a losing battle. When your well-being depends on someone else, you give away all of your power. A secure person won't want to carry this kind of burden and it can push him or her away.

Learn to silence your inner critic and practice self-compassion, and retrain yourself to focus on the aspects of yourself you like instead of the ones you don't like will help you build self-esteem quicker.

Enjoy the new positive you that comes with genuinely liking yourself, and a healthy self-confidence is an attractive quality that makes anyone want to be closer to you.

3. Establish a healthy independence.

Maintaining your sense of self-identity and taking care of your needs for personal well-being are the keys to keeping a healthy balance in a relationship. When you aren't dependent on your relationship to fill all of your needs, you feel more secure about your life. Being an independent person who has things going on outside of the relationship also makes you a more interesting and attractive partner.

4. Trust in yourself

Feeling secure in a relationship depends on trusting the other person but, more importantly, on learning to trust *yourself*. Trust yourself to know that no matter what the other person does, *you* will take care of *you*.

Trust yourself to know that you won't ignore your inner voice when it tells you that something isn't right. Trust yourself not to hide your feelings, trust yourself to make sure your needs are met, and trust yourself that you won't lose your sense of self-identity.

Trust yourself to know that if the relationship isn't working, you will be able to leave and still be a wholly functioning individual. When you trust yourself, feeling secure is almost a guarantee. It isn't necessary to be perfect in order to be in a happy, healthy, and secure relationship. We all come with some baggage. Trust yourself, love yourself and honor yourself.

God has given you all you need. HE APPROVED you already. Walk in it!

7
Bones of Self-Loathing
James 3:16

For where envy and self-seeking exist, confusion and every evil thing are there

****

Self-loathing is that underlying feeling that we are just not good enough for r anything or anyone. We can be subtle about our self-loathing or we may habitually compare ourselves to others. Finding fault with ourselves and putting ourselves down, looking at others as if they are superior to us. We listen intently to our critical inner voice while it scolds us; we allow our voice to berate us based on the lives of others we are comparing ourselves too.

We may try to suppress the feelings of inadequacy by behaving as though we are superior to others; more intelligent, more intuitive, or more attractive. It's as though we have to prove that we are the absolute best in order to avoid the torrent of internal abuse waiting to pounce the moment we show any fallibility.

However it comes about the self-loathing process is indicative of us as humans; of how we view ourselves in reality and then internally or should I say how we view ourselves from our heart.

The Causes of Self-Loathing

The causes of self-loathing lie in our past and how when, as children, we were trying to cope with our environment and those people in our lives the best way possible.

Our parents, like all of us, have mixed feelings toward themselves; they have things they like about themselves and they have self-critical thoughts and feelings. But the same negative feelings that parents have toward themselves they will often direct those feelings toward their children. If these parents have not resolved the trauma or loss they have experience, the child becomes the wall mount.

When a parent has unresolved feelings from the past, this will impact his or her reactions to his or her children. A parent who is sensitive to negative circumstances and pain typically affects their family in ways that causes damage to their lens of the world around them. When parents are stressed and filled with negative emotions, this will typically create a hostile environment. When hostility and stress are present; children who are typically afraid will turn inward and shut down to exhibiting emotions. Other children will stop identifying as helpless children and will act verbally and physically aggressive toward others like their parents.

So with humans being very fallible, we have all been subjected to situations and times in which we were made to feel like we were somehow inferior, inadequate, or desperately needing to prove otherwise. When we're newborns, we're fully, completely, unapologetically ourselves. We didn't beat ourselves up over belly fat, baldness or the moods. We didn't relate to the negative emotion behind those thoughts. We explored life with joy and curiosity, happy to be equipped with fingers, toes and eyes. Then when we began to grow, we're overwhelmed with the thoughts and messages that we are not good enough, or smart enough, pretty enough, funny enough, or whatever the enough is we are full of it.

The truth is, each of us is a flake of imperfection. Feeling better about ourselves is just a matter of remembering how amazing we really are. Some people have the misfortune to have been born to abusive parents who belittled them and prevented them from developing a healthy self-esteem. Some are born to see themselves in a negative light because of their physical appearance, a disability, or being too small or overweight. It has been said that it is difficult to be happy without liking oneself. But I ask the question, how can one learn to like oneself when one doesn't know oneself?

WHAT DO WE DISLIKE ABOUT OURSELVES?

People filled with self-loathing typically imagine that they dislike every part of themselves. If asked what it is they dislike, there will be a list of things, such as their physical appearance, their inability to excel academically or their inability to accomplish their dreams.

Why do self-loathers so readily overlook what is good about them? The answer is the boulder of pressure and lack of self-love they carry around. People who dislike themselves may acknowledge that they have positive attributes but any emotional impacts of these attributes have simply been blotted out.

Learning to like oneself is no easy task, especially when the foundation of self-loathing is a lack of self-love. And when there is no self-love, most of the time is spent entering into toxic and deflating relationships that validate our loathing behavior. But one must decide to change this self-loathing behavior in order to live a life of inner peace and joy. But, before change can occur, one must revisit the cause of this behavior. One must look at the circumstances that lead to self-hatred.

For example, your parents may have failed to praise you or support your accomplishments in school when you were young, they may have even ignored you which led you to conclude they didn't care about you, and this thought process led you to conclude you're not worth caring about. It's this last idea, not the memory of your parents ignoring you, but the memory of you believing you are not worthy. This powerful thought will make you loathe yourself if not checked by adult reasoning early on.

Once a narrative of worthlessness embeds itself in one's mind, it becomes extraordinarily difficult to disbelieve it, especially when one can find evidence that it represents a true account. But a narrative is just that: a story we tell ourselves. It may very well contain elements of truth that we are unattractive, that we fail a lot of the time, but to proceed from facts such as these to the conclusion that we deserve only our own perception is a significant thought error.

THE TRUE SOURCE OF SELF-ESTEEM

A self-loathing person does not respond to external praise well, they either will minimize it, explaining it away, or dismiss it altogether. It does not matter how many times their friends and families tell him or her that they are a good person, they will shrug it off, saying that these people obviously don't know the real person inside. The only way a self-loathing person is going to overcome his self-loathing is internally, changing their beliefs about themselves. And this is where self-compassion seems promising, especially if self-compassion can help the self-loathing person see himself differently. We shape our self-esteem in things about ourselves we perceive as unique: typically our looks, our skills, or our accomplishments and/or what others think we are. But we only need to experience the loss of any one of these supportive elements to recognize the danger of relying on them to create our self-esteem. Looks, as we all know, fade. Unwanted weight is often gained. Illness sometimes strikes, preventing us from running as fast, concentrating as hard, or thinking as clearly as we once did. Past accomplishments lose their ability to sustain us the farther into the past we have to look for them. We should aim to base our esteem on positive qualities that require no comparison to the qualities of others for us to value them. We must generate the wisdom and compassion to care for others until we've turned ourselves, piece by piece, into the people we most want to be.

If we want to like ourselves we have to earn our own respect. Luckily, doing this doesn't require that we become people of extraordinary physical attractiveness or accomplishment. It only requires we become people of extraordinary character the one thing we all can do regardless of background.

Treating others well, it turns out, is the fastest path to a healthy self-esteem. If you dislike yourself, stop focusing on your negative qualities. We all have negative things about us that we wish were not there so there's nothing special about *your* negativity. But if you focus instead on caring for others, I guarantee the more you'll be able to care about yourself.

Self-Loathing is not your conscience, that underlies self-loathing but more often than not it is your critical inner voice. For instance, it may tell you about things you are doing that are not in your interest, just like your conscience does. But this process is diametrically opposed to your self-interest. Whereas your conscience will tell you not to have that one drink too many, this process first lures you into taking that drink and then attacks you viciously for having taken it. Your conscience may nag at you to revisit a conversation in which you may have not been kind and to offer up an apology for your rude behavior. But the internal enemy either justifies your having been rude by attacking the other person, *He deserved it, he is such a jerk!* Or berates you furiously for your part, *you are always so touchy and mean. No wonder no one likes you!*

How to Overcome Self-Loathing

Do the difficult things while they are easy and do the great things while they are small. A journey of a thousand miles must begin with a single step.

Lao Tzu

We may all agree that we want to change how we feel and look at ourselves. We may even know that we must take the first step to healing but when we are self-loathers, we are held back by the battle in our minds on whether we believe the first step to being proud of oneself is worth taking. No matter what circumstances you find yourself in, a nasty point of view toward yourself is never warranted. It is never in your self-interest. The proper viewpoint toward yourself should be one of friendship. Think about yourself and treat yourself as you would a close friend; respectfully and with affection.

You are powerful in your own right; free to choose any point of view or course of action available to you. Any outer voice that defines you, either tearing you down, *you are such an idiot!* Or building you up, *you're the smartest one in this school!* is attempting to take away your power and freedom. You must be your own advocate, taking your own side in your life.

There are many avenues through which to address the issue of self-loathing. First, just by becoming aware that a division exists within us allows for a more rational, reasonable assessment of events in our daily lives. Once we have identified this process as being different from honest self-reflection, we are then able to think more objectively about ourselves and the various situations we encounter.

When we honestly look into our selves we will see that the foundation to self-loathing is our lack of self-forgiveness. Self-forgiveness unlike forgiveness of others typically escapes the loather. They don't recognize the need to forgive oneself because they can only validate that they are not good enough instead of grasping hold to the things that are wonderful about them.

In the face of self-forgiveness the once difficult task of forgiven others becomes digestible because we tend to think others have more value than we do. When we forgive others we may struggle with being good to them even though they are not good to us but we do it. When it comes to forgiving ourselves we are not so accommodating. We tend to justify why we don't deserve self-forgiveness and live out our self-induced life sentence.

Some loathers have a very difficult time maintaining relationships due to their feeling so inadequacy. The loather will feel they are not worthy enough to receive love and intimacy in a relationship or they may feel that their need s are not important and will not impose their needs on their love ones.

Challenging our tendency toward self-loathing is one of the most valuable uses of our time and energy. We can change the course of our perception by changing how we see ourselves and by accepting the dynamic person we are in spite of our flaws. We all have flaws but they should not be over magnified in our lives to the point that we despise oneself. As we extricate ourselves from this inimical process, we become free to experience ourselves and the lives we are living from a kindly and empowered perspective.

Prayer

Father,

Your word says in Ephesians 4:23 that we are to be continually renewed in the spirit of your mind (a fresh, untarnished mental attitude). I haven't done right by myself with the thoughts I have had toward myself.

I have carried a yoke of self-depreciation, sabotage, being critical of myself and lacking confidence in who I am. I have allowed the burdens of life to choke me to the point I don't see myself as a person deserving of love, value or respect.

I ask that you forgive me for not cherishing the masterpiece you made when I was created. I am not the circumstances of my conception. I release all thoughts of could not, am not, was not, should not, am not worthy, am not lovely, am not enough.

I renew my thoughts and mind with healing words and speak life to the areas that have been dead.

    I am enough
    I am worthy
    I am love
    I am redeemed and restored
    I was created to do great things

Date:_____

8
Bones of Barren Emotions
Isaiah 44:3

For I will pour out water to quench your thirst and to irrigate your parched fields.

****

Barren: Not producing or incapable of producing, unproductive; unfruitful: **barren** land. Without capacity to interest or attract:

Emotional Barren is the experience of feeling disconnected, surreal, and unable to feel emotions. Individuals will feel empty and numb, and it seems as if you are an outside observer of your own life.

You may also report feeling a loss of control over your thoughts or action. Sometimes these circumstances can leave us feeling emotionally empty. Being emotionally empty doesn't make us a bad person; we are far from being a bad person. We typically have become emotionally barren/bankrupt due to allowing life to empty out of us or our emotional tanks having long since been depleted by disappointments, rejections and/or abandonment.

We can determine if we are emotionally barren by answering the following questions. Being true to yourself is critical, so be honest to yourself no matter how hard .

Do you experience any of the following?

Do you feel detached from family and friends, often feeling like you have no one?

Do you look at yourself and see a different person?

Is there joy and laughter missing from your life?

Do you withhold affection or push away from affection?

Do you deny others the opportunity to pour into you?

Are you stuck in grief and/or heartbreak

Life can deal us some very hard blows, it can bring situations across our paths to alert us or it can completely take our breath away. Most of us will continue to battle through life unexpected without it taking our emotional life. There are those who have continued to receive back to back hurt, disappointment, rejection and/or abandonment which will completely empty out our emotions.

Relationships can be extremely hard especially romantic relationships, where you have two adults from different backgrounds, individual opinions and separate perceptions merging together to be one. He wants her to be his ideal and she wants him to be her dream. This makes for a very challenging relationship and when you throw in that one of the individuals is emotionally bankrupt you have a recipe for a dysfunctional, frustrating and exhausting relationship.

When a person is emotionally bankrupt, there is no place from which they can draw love, kindness, empathy and any number of other emotions that it takes to sustain a healthy relationship. Even their communication is rehearsed; a damaged perspective often skews their logic

The following are some signs that you may be or are dealing with an emotional bankrupt person:

1. Angry – When a person is mad about everything, it is a sure sign of deeper issues. If you notice a person has an excessive amount of hot buttons, it means they are too full of rage to send positive emotions your way. Anger and love can't exist in the same space.
2. Self-Centered Behavior – If a person is always saying "me, me, me," you know the type; every conversation, scenario or activity must revolve around them.
3. Use Abusive Behavior – I'm not just talking physical abuse, we overlook verbal and emotional abuse because we don't always recognize it. Neglect is also abuse. When you or your significant other pulls a disappearing act, it's still abuse. You cant love pass this behavior or ignore it. This only tends to get worse as the time passes.

4. Laziness – If a person won't get a job, clean the house or take care of their own
   bodies, you can't expect them to put effort into caring for you?
5. Greed – A person of greed will never have enough of anything to fill
   them up. Money, clothes, shoes, food, they will continue to seek multiple things
   in abundance and move rapidly between acquisitions and people. For them, it's
   all about the process of getting more. They are never happy with what they
   have, which will also include you?
6. No Empathy – If a person can't relate to someone else's pain, they will
   have no qualms about causing it.
7. Control Freaks – A person who needs to control other people and scenarios are
   more prone to become abusive when they feel like they are losing control or
   can't manipulate the situation.
8. Hatred – People who harbor hate are closed off to anything different. They are
   extremely hostile and have no compassion for anyone else.

In order for us to steer clear of people who lack emotional health we have to be willing to check our own emotional compass. How do you respond to relational issues? How do you regulate your emotions? Are you impulsive, critical and/or judgmental? If you so you may possibly be emotional barren/ bankrupted.

Emotional Bankruptcy is when a person who does not know how to or is not able to express, process, share, show, accept, vocalize and/or deal with their emotions. Some examples of this could be a partner not saying "I love you or saying it yet emotionally does not show it". They may have an issue with hugging or kissing or showing affection. Or they may be able to do these things under the guise that if things get to intimate, too loveable, they will sabotage and back away. In most cases they find fault with their partner to use it to validate their in ability to have an emotional a connection.

Do you know someone who no matter how much you share your feelings with them and express your emotions or feelings, they either cannot or won't reciprocate? They may leave the room, ignore or avoid you or do other things to avoid sharing their feelings. They may act out passive aggressively. They can act out in revenge for things you have done to them, instead of telling you they are upset with you for what you did to them. Maybe I am describing you and how you behave and react to your own feelings and emotions. If this is you, then I am so glad you are reading this right now, because I hope this will help you to have a better life. If this is not you but someone you know, then this will definitely help you too.

This emotional bankruptcy is harmful to both the person not expressing their emotions as well as the person in a relationship with the emotionally bankrupt person.

First, emotional stress causes 98% of health problems and illness. Every time you do not accept the process, share or express your feelings and emotions, you are creating stress in your brain which is harming your entire body, mind and spirit. Your emotional bankruptcy is making you sick and possibly shortening your life.

When you are someone who is emotionally bankrupt and you are in a romantic relationship with someone, it can destroy the relationship/marriage. I know a woman who is very loving and affectionate, emotionally healthy and needs to receive love and affection in order to be happy. Unfortunately, she is married to a man who is emotionally bankrupt. He hides and chokes down all his emotions until he blows up with angry outbursts and acts out by taking all his anger over life out on his wife. He blames her for everything that has gone wrong in his life, despite the fact that she has been kind, loving and affectionate to him throughout their marriage. He never tells her "I love you" and has never even told her she is important to him or beautiful. He keeps all his feelings and emotions bottled up inside the way his parents taught him too. Both of his parents came from cultures where people do not express their emotions and if a boy or man expresses their emotions, it's a terrible thing. So instead he has volcanic eruptions of anger from time to time. The result of this man's emotional bankruptcy is that his wife who is very emotionally healthy feels unloved, disrespected, unwanted and most of all she is very unhappy in the relationship.

The emotions that she is dealing with and processing as a result of her partners bankruptcy are making her sick because even if you are an emotionally healthy person, being with someone who is emotionally bankrupt will make you very sick.

Here are a few tips to deal with emotional bankruptcy.

1. If you are someone who is brave enough to admit you have an issue with your emotions or may be bankrupt, then you need to get counseling immediately to learn how to process and express your emotions. If you continue on this way, you are making yourself sick and you are making your relatives and spouse sick too.

2. If you are an emotionally healthy person in a relationship with someone who is bankrupt, make them seek out counseling to change. If they are not willing to change, then assess what you absolutely need and decide if you can do without it. Other people are not responsible for your happiness, but at the same time if they are making you miserable it's not good.

3. If you are single, make sure to not enter serious relationships with people who are emotionally bankrupt. You are setting yourself up for major disappointment in your life.

4. If two people who are both emotionally bankrupt and are in a relationship not only will this be a very bad relationship filled with frustration, disappointment, anger and rejection..

An individual who is emotionally bankrupt has given out to others and needs to be refilled back up. It is time to pull back from what is causing this deficit in your life, or if you are surrounded by continual stressors in your life; you need to find some time to get alone with yourself and God. And exhale!!

If you are empty inside you cannot truly help others, we have to let God pour into our "empty cups,". If you are in ministry, have dysfunctional, unhealthy family, or are in a helping profession, there will be times you will need refreshing and time alone with God. It is not only okay to do so, but healthy emotionally, physically, and spiritually. There must be balance in your life to maintain health. If you are pouring out to others all the time, and never take time to get filled back up; all of your energy will be consumed. If you are not hearing from the Lord, you could possibly be operating in your flesh and not the Spirit of God.

What are some signs of being emotionally bankrupt?

1. Exhaustion, tired more than you feel rested.
2. Irritable, easily frustrated or provoked.
3. Easily offended.
4. Discouraged and possibly depressed.
5. Anxious and worried.
6. Forgetful.
7. Feel physically worn-down, headaches and weakened immune system.
8. Cannot settle down, mind is racing constantly.
9. Difficulty sleeping at night or wanting to sleep more.
10. Lack of peace and joy.
11. Not interested in activities with others. May even isolate.

What can you do if you are emotionally bankrupt?

1. Rest when needed.
2. Refresh with time alone with God.
3. Read from the book of Psalms in the Bible when you need to recharge.
4. Refocus on the things of God, not the circumstances.
5. Reexamine the things in your life that are causing constant stress.
6. Reach out to someone you can trust and allow them to pray for you.
7. Reconsider cutting down or back the things that are unhealthy in your life.
8. Renew your mind. Take every thought captive. Don't allow your mind to be used as

   a garbage dump by the enemy during stressful times.
9. Rejuvenate by taking warm baths to relax tired muscles.
10. Relax and do something just for you; have fun.

So what can you do if you think you may have been emotionally neglected as a child? Here are some tips:

1. Learn to be aware of positive and negative emotions when you're experiencing them.

If you've spent your life being disconnected from your feelings, the first step is to learn to identify positive and negative emotions. It's important to acknowledge your feelings, its ok to say you are angry, or sad. You may not even have words for how you feel, which is perfectly normal if you didn't grow up in a home where people talked about their feelings.

2. Identify your needs, and take steps to meet them.

Many people who experienced emotional neglect is often unaware of what they need and typically don't feel deserving in regards to getting their needs met. It is important to develop your emotional vocabulary by researching emotions. Once you know what you need, it's time to take action.

3. Be gentle with and take good care of yourself, starting with small steps.

People who experience emotional neglect often have difficulty with Self-Care and are unaware of their feelings and needs, they frequently don't know where to start. Try treating yourself with the same care and gentleness you would give to other who wasn't able to take care of themselves or who needed you during a difficult time in their life. Be tender and nice to yourself, especially if you tend to be self-critical or judgmental.

And remember: Rome wasn't built in a day! This is a process. When you skin your knee, you need to clean out the wound and expose it to the light of day; the same holds true for emotional wounds. Dare to bring the wound out of hiding, give it some light and air, and you'll be on the road to healing.

A Dream Deferred

by

Langston Hughes

What happens to a dream deferred?
Does it dry up like a raisin in the sun?
Or fester like a sore-- And then run?
Does it stink like rotten meat?
Or crust and sugar over-- like a syrupy sweet?
Maybe it just sags like a heavy load.
Or does it explode?

Having to postpone one's deepest desires can lead to destruction. What happens to a dream deferred? A dream is a goal in life as well as dreams experienced during sleep. The dream of goals and/or accomplishments is important to the dreamer's life. Any important dream or goal that must be delayed can have serious negative effects.

The danger in delaying out dreams makes it easy to shelve them forever. We tend to forget about our dreams because we are helping someone else make their dreams come true. We have to believe in our own self and our dream and value the opportunity that life gives us in making dreams come true.

Every day that you awake is another opportunity to take a step toward your dream. Whether it is creating a dream board or writing down things that need to be completed in order for you to have your dream.

The only dreams that come true are the ones that you chase. Don't let fear or other people convince you that you can't do it or that it is not the time to do it. No matter how big your dream is, believe in it and work it. No one else can live and work YOUR dream.

Don't dream your life,
Live your Dreams

Your Vision

Make a covenant with yourself and write down the steps that you need to take to accomplish your visions. We are more than conquerors and can achieve whatever we set our minds to doing.

We can no longer allow procrastination, old wounds or old thought patterns to keep us from doing what we are purposed to do. If you honestly answered and completed the assignments in this book, then you should no longer allow old thoughts and patterns to hinder you.

Go after you vision and don't stop until you have achieved all you set to do…

We got this, Let's Go!!!!

■■■

Write down your vision for the next 5 years, be specific and touch every area in your life.

Personal

Spiritual

Physically

Emotionally

Romantically

Friendships

Personal

Spiritual

Physical

Made in the USA
Columbia, SC
14 February 2020